HEEL MY HEART
MY STRUT 2 SUCCESS

R. NIKKI CHANEY

Copyright © 2016 R. Nikki Chaney

All rights reserved.

ISBN:069254674X
ISBN-13: : 978-0-692-54674-1

DEDICATION

I dedicate this book to all of our sisters whom we have lost to this epidemic and to all of us who are fighting, fought and declared victory over domestic violence and abuse. This is for my Survivors.

ACKNOWLEDGMENTS

Special acknowledgments to my husband, Ken "Dirt" Chaney, our kids & family. Acknowledgment to Dale Trimble for the remarkable book cover.

My Strut 2 Success

A self-help journal created for victims of domestic violence and abuse to journey their steps towards "heeling their broken heart."

Introduction:

What is domestic violence and abuse? The dictionary term is simple and easy for us all to understand.

Definition. Domestic violence and emotional abuse are behaviors used by one person in a relationship to control the other. Partners may be married or not married; heterosexual, gay, or lesbian; living together, separated or dating.

Now let's break that down. What are emotional behaviors? Emotional behavior is a psychological state that arises spontaneously rather than through conscious effort and is sometimes accompanied by physiological changes; a feeling.

A further break down. What is control? Control is to exercise authoritative or dominating influence over; direct.

It's set. We are educated on domestic violence and abuse, right? Sure we are. The definitions are here at our fingertips, on Google or any other book or electronic source that provides us with a definitive meaning.

The objective of this self-help book is to identify our problem and prepare for the journey ahead. No more silence. No more hiding. No more excuses. It's time to take back our lives and live the abundant life that God has promised. It's time to Heel Our Heart.

The Beginning

If you have gotten past the introduction and are asking yourself, "why is the Author speaking in first person, then adjust your seat because it's time to take the mask off." I, too, was a victim of domestic violence and abuse and even after writing and publishing two novels that disclosed my personal encounters, I have yet to "Heel My Heart." This journey is for us. Read, discuss and take notes. We will continue on this journey together. In the introduction, I gave the dictionary meaning of domestic violence and emotional abuse, emotional behaviors, and the definition of control. What these terms mean to you is what's important. They all have different meanings for us that have been through or going through domestic violence and abuse. I will focus on what they mean to me. Here's a Flashback Friday or Throwback Thursday, our generational terms for something that is old. I sat in my favorite place in the house, the upstairs closet. Now this wasn't just a closet to me. This was a place of peace, comfort, and a place where I could express my feelings. Now I know that you may have had imaginary friends, but I believed that my friends were actually real. I had a voice with them. They listened and I listened to them. We were besties. Most nights I would go in there right after I showered, right before bed time. I would always tell my friends to get ready because we are going to hear the knocking and the yelling. What's the knocking and the yelling, you may ask? Well I knew it to be a moment when my parents would close the door for hours at a time and began whispering and then began yelling. I later found that to be a sound of erotic affection. When I wasn't hearing the knocking and the yelling, I would hear the curse words and the breaking of glass and the crying of a woman, my mother. Every time that I got in my closet, I always had something to look forward to from my parents. Parents. I use that term loosely because my mother's boyfriend assumed the responsibility of my absent father. My father was unknown to me. My mother began a relationship with my step-father when I was around three years old. I didn't mind having a man around. It actually kept my mom occupied. My age during this period was around six. I had always heard my mom crying and I've seen fear in her eyes countless times that I can remember even before the age of three. Around the age of two, vaguely remembering that had to be my age because I was talking and it was before my mom began dating my current step-father, I remembered the same fear in her eyes as she held me against her and yelled and cried as her then boyfriend stabbed a knife through the door that she was leaning hard against to keep him out. I don't remember crying but I do remember being scared. These years are what I feel were detrimental. Years of knocking, yelling, cursing and crying continued until I was around 12 or 13. I remembered one night while holding my teddy bear, the bear that I began to be erotic with, hearing a loud clunk. I yelled down to the bottom bunk to ask my sister what was going on. Okay, let's take it back. Yes, I have a sister that is two years older than me. Speed forward. We realized that another fight was in progress. We knew that a fight would probably break out because when we arrived home from school earlier that day, we noticed the cut off straws on the table. My sister was adamant about helping my mom anytime that my step-father would hit her. I would just sit numb, not knowing what to say or do. I never understood why I was so emotionless. That was the last night that my mom stayed in that relationship. She packed up my sister and me and the whole house and we moved. Here's something that I want you to do so that I don't lose you throughout my rambling. Whenever you read something that stimulates your senses, think about why you have an emotional attachment to what you are reading. If something strikes you as common to your childhood, underline it. At the end of this chapter, jot down your emotions, feelings or even chart moments of your childhood that may have been disturbing. Remember we are doing this together. Speeding along. I was excited to finally be in a new town. I wasn't unfamiliar with this area; we frequent this area and had family here as well. It was just different to be living here now. My mom continued many relationships, some of the guys I knew and some of them, I just knew of. We had guys over to the house all of the time. One night my mom had friends over and this guy snuck in her room. , the same exact room where I was sleeping. I felt someone climbing under the sheets and then I saw a big Afro and the silhouette of a man. I started to yell but he silenced me. He began to fondle me. I asked him to stop over and over again. He started to pull my panties down and I kicked him and yelled for my mom. She never came. The music was too loud. Out of fear that my mom would catch him, he jumped up and left. This moment was embarrassing but I used it as an opportunity to brag to my friends that a man wanted me. I always bragged to my friends about sex and how much of it I was having. It was all a lie. I was only 14 years old. I was still a virgin. I was the only 9th grade girl that wasn't having sex. A lot of guys attempted to care for me until they could get me in bed and I would freeze up and become extremely paranoid so nothing would ever happen. Grown men even wanted to be with me. I had one grown man that would come pick me up late hours when my mom would be on her second job. He never wanted sex, however, just my company. When I entered my sophomore year in high school, I rekindled an old romance that I had with my first boyfriend when I was 12 years old. He was a senior and he also had a girlfriend. He treated me better though. He wanted to have sex with me and not her so in my mind, I was the one that he would rather be with. One summer morning, after a whole school year of promising my goodies to this guy, it finally happened. I had officially lost my virginity. I was so happy to hear my own knocks and yells. The knocking was the headboard and the yells were the pain/pleasure. I finally knew what it was like to be loved. He was leaving for the Navy and I was going to be his girl, at least that's what I thought. After another erotic moment, he left me. He began a long lasting relationship with another girl. I couldn't believe that this was happening. I finally give him something that every guy wanted and he rejected me. Not only would he leave me, but he would also leave a dirty image to our entire high school about me, since he told everyone about the dirty, red bed sheets. He would also leave a girl broken, in search of true love.

I'll end this chapter asking these questions: Was abuse identified in my mother's relationship? Was abuse identified from the absence of my father? Was abuse identified from the bedroom predator? Was abuse identified from my first lover?

All of this contributed to a long lasting cycle that I didn't even recognize as a problem or as the definitions for the terms listed above. Can you relate to any of my circumstances detailed above? Definitions and terms are hard to identify when you need to apply them to a problem.

R. NIKKI CHANEY

HEEL MY HEART: MY STRUT 2 SUCCESS

The Journey Continues

Many times, we as women need a man to validate our being. This statement means, in a nutshell, you need a man to make you feel like a woman. But why? Based off of an article entitled, "The Underlying Reasons Why Some Women NEED Male Approval In Order To Feel Validated!" by Grace M. Williams, she explains it by this, "Even though the average postmodern woman is fierce and highly independent, there are still some women who need men in order to validate their being. They strongly contend that men are superior to them. It is their assertion that because men are superior, whatever the man says is equivalent to an imprimatur.

There are women who subvert their identities to please their boyfriends, significant others, and/or husbands. They feel that as women, they are somewhat inconsequential so their opinions and wants mean absolutely nothing at all. They believe that the man should have the uppermost hand in the relationship because this was somehow preordained."

After reading this opinion by Grace, can you identify with these characteristics that are presented? Most women, suffering from domestic violence and abuse can relate to this.

Let's continue on our journey and remember to journey your steps in the blank pages after each chapter and continue underlining statements and events that Scream out to you.

Finally after creating a series of "knocking and yelling" scenes with so many boys, I met one that I would soon bear children with. He was my first love. Mind you, I experienced an episode previously with someone I considered to be my first love, but my emotional attachment to this one was different. I showed him that I could be all the woman that he has never experienced or fathomed. I bought him clothes, sexed him on the regular and even assumed the role as a mother to his infant child. Giving all of this, I knew he would never mistreat me in the way that my "first love" did. Our first year was blissful and it would also be the year that we conceived our first born child. During my pregnancy would also be the first time that I would see "love" as I grew to know it. Nights full of more knocking and yelling but this time it wasn't pleasurable. The knocks were him hitting me or me throwing something at him and glass shattering. The yelling was screams for help. After each altercation, he would cry and beg for my forgiveness and promise not to do it again. I've never seen someone so sincere in an apology towards me. I felt more loved after each altercation that I looked forward to the next altercation so that he could make me feel loved all over again. For years the abuse continued. After 6 years and 3 kids later, I managed to walk away. My last son was forcefully conceived and in that moment, I realized how weak I was for him and how strong I had to be for these three little boys that only had me for survival.

After many years of physical, mental and sexual abuse I lost my identity as a woman. I didn't know who I was or what I deserved or how I deserved to be treated. I entered multiple sexual relationships and I say sexual because that's all I gave and all that was reciprocated. But why did love look like this to me? Why couldn't I determine early on that this behavior was unacceptable? Why did I enjoy the "break ups to make ups?" Why did I have an attraction to abuse? Earlier it was stated that all victims experience different types of abuse. So far, I've endured sexual, emotional, and physical abuse. These abusive behaviors are very common to women affected by domestic violence and abuse. These behaviors have a cycle that generally continues. I'm not saying that people cannot change, however I'm saying that the ways of "man" are unknown. One time is more than enough. It's no need to stick around for multiple occasions. Staying in these types of relationships for too long are very unhealthy. Please view the cycle wheel:

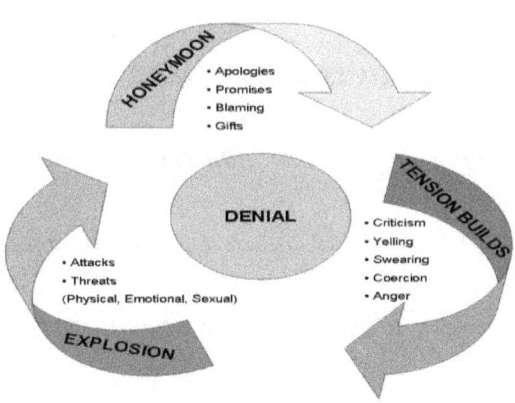

Can you identify with this cycle? How many relationships have you been in that resembles the acts on the wheel? Well so far, I had two relationships. The first one was at 16 and lasted for a short period of time but before I knew it, I had attracted another guy who would take it a bit further and that violence would last over eight years. I couldn't seem to break away. Even after our last child was born, my connection to this man couldn't be broken. What's in an abused woman that keeps her going back to her abuser? In an article composed on www.crisisconnectioninc.org, it states this, "Fact: Most victims of domestic violence leave their abusers, often several times. It may take a number of attempts to permanently separate because abusers use violence, financial control, or threats about the children, to compel victims to return. Additionally, a lack of support from friends, family members, or professionals, such as court personnel, law enforcement officers, counselors, or clergy members, may cause victims to return. Since the risk of further violence often increases after victims separate from their abusers, it can be even harder for victims to leave if they cannot obtain effective legal relief. Victims who receive appropriate legal assistance at an early stage increase their chances of obtaining the protection and financial security they need to leave their abusers permanently. While some victims may become involved with other partners who later begin to abuse them, there is no evidence that the majority of victims have this experience.

And if all of the above were not reason enough to return, consider the following likely problems:

Reactions to abuse: Victims of abuse are often full of intense and often conflicting emotions. People that have not been in an abusive relationship cannot understand how you can still love or care about someone that abuses you: she did not become involved with a monster and even now he isn't always cruel, he is still extremely kind between his ugliness and attacks. Emotions cannot be turned on or off like a light. You can feel quite torn between loving the person and being afraid of them. You may *experience all feelings listed or just a few. Sometimes feelings may flow from one to another and back again. Holding on to (and not be allowed to escape) negative emotions slowly kills the spirit."*

We will end our journey here. Answer the questions that were asked during this section and don't forget to highlight those areas that "scream" out to you?

What have been some reasons for you staying in an abusive relationship? I left one just to enter another one. Stay focused and we will determine why abused women are attracted to the same type of men. We are nearing a great experience. Keep your heels on as we continue this journey.

Still High Stepping

Now in my late 20's, I had endured my share of abusive relationships. Around the age of 25, I had finally rebuilt enough to love me first and remain single until God sent me the perfect man. To me, the perfect man would be a God fearing man, a great father figure, provider, and more than anything loved me like God loved The Church. The First Sunday in June, coincidentally, I met an amazing man during church service. I was overwhelmed by his masculinity and he was groomed so nicely. His suit was a perfect fit and he was wearing an attractive fragrance. After church he *came to shake my hand. I didn't know why at that moment but a couple of months later we became a hot couple. Here's a little background about my knight and shining armor. He was about 5'9, 165 pounds, with skin as light as the sun on a bright sunny day. He was 9 years older than me but was still able to maintain my frisky tendencies. What was so amazing was that he was financially stable. He drove trucks for a living, had invested in property and lived quite nicely. I wasn't thrilled that he had a family, two kids, both girls, one 15 and one 7 but at least the girls were capable of taking care of themselves and school ready.*

I won't dwell or put much emphasis on this relationship because I have learned through therapy that the more you dwell on things that break your spirit, the more those things will control you. On that note, if you are dwelling on incidents that you are remembering through this process, stop now and say this prayer with me, "Lord help me to close the doors of regret behind me, knowing that You have already gone ahead, preparing even greater opportunities for me. Let me not spend so much time looking back that I cannot see the new doors already waiting for me to come up and knock again. I thank You for the chances that You give me over and over again to ask and receive from Your hand of love and mercy, Amen." I love this prayer. It comes from this awesome Prayer Book that I purchased years ago entitled "Becoming A Woman of Worth" Prayer Book, written by Karen Moore. If you haven't purchased it, you can find it at your local Publix grocery store or Walgreens.

I feel great after that prayer. How do you feel? Well, to continue just a little more so that you can see just how awesome God is and so that you could recognize yet another slip that I had in my heels and how I was able to get up and keep strutting. The first sign that this man was really not God sent was one incident after being together for only four months. I can remember putting my *phone on the charger in my truck because I couldn't find my house charger and he popped up at my house since I didn't answer when he called. I was shocked to see him on my doorstep. He yelled at me and acted irrational because of me not only answering my phone but because I didn't come to church that night. He made sure to frighten me just enough to not have that happen again. I, of course, felt like he was just whipped and wanted me around all of the time so I ignored the number one sign of abuse, Control. Shortly after that, in our relationship, he said that it was hard for him to pay my bills and his so he suggested, well nearly forced me to move out of my apartment and move in with him. It was a convincing speech so I packed up me and my boys and moved with him. Not only was this a form of control but also a way to keep watch over my every move, but once again, it was something that I ignored because I was now out of poverty and I could offer my boys a more stable environment. After being out of my comfort zone for a little over a month, I began to feel a sense of* discomfort. I wasn't happy going to sleep and waking up with the same person every day. I felt forced into something that I didn't want to be in. I felt like my independence was gone and when I used to have a say so of cleaning or not, cooking or not, I no longer controlled, I had to, no exceptions. Realizing my feelings, I decided to approach them. I spoke on how I was feeling and he said that he understood so I began to plan my exit. It was like a weight had lifted off of my shoulders. I still had my job so I was able to save enough money to move out within a month. The day before I was expected to move, he walked in and proposed. I was taken aback. Why would he propose when I clearly expressed that I wasn't even ready to be "live in partners," here he was proposing "lifetime partners." I didn't want to hurt his feelings, so I said yes.

Okay, ladies. How many of you have felt like you were trapped in a situation like this? How did you handle it? Were you *uncomfortable with your decision? Why? Take a moment to reflect and don't forget to utilize the blank pages to jot down your answers and thoughts.*

Continuing on this journey, we continued to live happily, that was until my boys' father came back in the picture. For almost a year he kept us away from him. I didn't realize at the moment when he asked for me to move in with him that he was also hiding us from the boys' father. Their father was in jail when my fiancé and I began dating and since we were on such awful terms when he was incarcerated, I was glad to move with this new man. I did explain to my fiancé that every relationship that I was involved in, that my ex, the boys' father would come back into my life and I would leave whomever and go back to him. It wasn't until one day that I was contacted by a relative of mine who told me that the boys' father wanted my number so that he could get in contact with his kids, that I knew this man was in fact hiding us from him. I told him about it and he immediately freaked out. He had to be around when I was on the phone with him and he was adamant about knowing the details about every conversation that we had outside of his presence. I felt like I had no control over my business, because it was in fact my business to deal with any issues that arises with the father of my kids. My fiancé didn't agree. I was so burden down with explaining my every move concerning my boys' father with my fiancé that I just cut ties with him and changed my number. My fiancé was happy about my decision. This still wasn't enough for me to leave. We had been engaged now for almost a year so I began to plan our wedding. During the planning, one night during dinner, I picked up my phone to scroll through it for a number and had noticed that a guy friend of mine's number had been dialed. That was strange because I would never call him being that I was in a committed relationship and him and I was romantically involved. I asked my fiancé did he call the number and he said yes and that he felt bad because a guy and his girlfriend was on the answer machine. I told him who the guy was, in fact, and he got angry. I was angry because he went through my phone and I didn't appreciate him invading my privacy that way. He was angry because he said this is a new phone so you had to purposely add this guy's number. He began to question me and told me to get out of his house. He didn't throw my kids out, however, but he pushed me down the stairs in the middle of winter and threw my belongings on top of me. I was confused, angry, disappointed and suddenly afraid of the man that I was planning to marry. I packed up my kids the next day and left. I didn't want to tell anyone because I didn't want them to know that I was in another abusive relationship. He wasn't hitting me but he was mentally and verbally abusing me, which to me is worse. I didn't want to go back to the boys' father either because everyone was expecting that to happen. My family and friends had said from the beginning that I would mess up this good relationship in order to go back to someone who was no good for me. I thought hard about my decision, well actually an ultimatum. My fiancé told me that if I wasn't back at home by the time he returned from work that it would be over for good, so I packed up my kids once again and went back to my abuser.

Ok ladies. I have learned through this process that the reason that I have endured these abusive relationships was for one or three reasons. Reason 1: Financial stability. Reason 2: Fear. Reason 3: Embarrassment. What are your reasons? Whatever you're reasoning, you must know that the person that you see every day in the mirror is not happy within. No matter how much makeup you have on, it will never cover the hurt within. Never be bullied into staying into a situation that's uncomfortable. It's fine to talk about your hurts and disappointments. It will actually make you feel good. If you can't talk to family, seek a counselor or someone through your church or an organization that helps women *affected by domestic violence and abuse. To my knowledge, it's many organizations that are ready to assist you. There will be some listed in the back of this book for your convenience. Ladies don't forget to record all of your answers and thoughts on the blank pages provided.*

Let's continue on this journey. The day finally came. I was about to be a married woman. This was a fairytale wedding. Log cabins, horse and carriages, white doves and a host of family and friends joined us for this special occasion. Imagine for a moment ladies, what's your "dream wedding?" If you are currently married, did you have the wedding of your dreams? I would have to answer, yes. This was perfect and in that moment, I forgot about the control, the mental abuse, and the fact that this man would probably continue with this behavior even after such a beautiful ceremony. It was nearly five months after our blissful ceremony that I began to notice a change in my husband. He began to distant himself and talked very cold to me. I questioned my behaviors. I went over and beyond to please him because I was convinced that I was the cause of his attitude. Nothing I did worked. One day he went and purchased a gun. I was afraid of guns so I wasn't sure why he would buy such a dangerous weapon. He would play with it in front of me, cock and shoot it in my presence and basically smirk an evil smirk every time that I would cringe. He even proposed that I learn how to shoot it. I was opposed to this but for him, I complied. One day he began to ask me questions like would I ever leave him? I didn't know where the questions came from but I assured him that I would never leave him. He was sitting in front of me on the floor next to our bedside when he pulled out the gun. I rubbed my eyes and sat up a little to adjust my eyes and noticed that he in fact had his gun pointed in my direction. I was stunned and horrified. Before I could speak, he cocked the gun and asked me the same question again, would I ever leave him. This time my voice was cracking but I replied the same answer. He replied, "If you ever leave me there will be a body bag between both of us." After placing the fear of life in me, he got up and left. Ladies have you ever experienced this type of mental abuse? This type of abuse has a longing affect. Not only was I afraid but his words constantly lingered in my thoughts. Daily thoughts of escaping crossed my mind. I didn't know how to feel or what to think. I was married. What would God think of my decision to leave my husband? I never studied God's Word or even prayed I just took matters in my own hands. I thought that if I had an affair with the man that he had befriended, which was my boys' father, then he would definitely divorce me. It never crossed my mind that he would kill me if I committed such an act because he said for me to never leave him, not the other way around. My mind was programmed to believing in this plan so I executed it. I had an affair and told my husband shortly after. He responded in a way totally different than I expected. He called my ex and asked him about the day in question and to my surprise my ex denied the accusations. He then pulled my bank records and didn't notice a gas station or hotel room for the location that I indicated the incident. He was convinced that I was lying and was just trying to find a reason to leave him. He made another phone call and afterwards told me to get dress in all white. I was confused but I done as I was told. We left the house and headed in the direction of our church. When we arrived, our Pastor greeted us at the door. My husband told the Pastor that I needed to get baptized. I was still looking confused but I didn't say anything. After we left, I asked him why he was putting on all of these charades and he replied, "You are clean now and no one has been on top of you." I was blown away and realized that I was stuck with this man forever. Ladies this was a most terrifying experience to go through. Needless to say a huge turn events occurred after that. My husband threatened suicide as an attempt to get me to stay with him. I wanted to save him. How many time ladies have your maternal *instincts kicked in? How many times have your nurturing instincts kicked in? We as women were born to nurture and those instincts tend to kick in with anyone that we love or care for. We want to save them and are convinced at times that if we love harder that we will save them. Ladies never stay with a person that threatens self-harm. If they are willing to harm themselves, it would be nothing for them to harm you. If this happens you need to quickly try to deescalate the situation and call the police. If you are able to leave, do so and don't return. I can't stress this enough. Please don't stay and don't return.*

I stayed and wanted to save him. He told me that our Pastor told him that it was a devil in me that exited my body and attacked him. I believed him and prayed for these demons to leave my soul. As you read this, jot down your thoughts and email me your feelings about how you think I handled this situation? Do you think I was crazy for thinking that I had internal demons? I really would like to know your opinions.

Months later my husband couldn't bear the fact of me wanting a divorce so he did the unthinkable. He kidnapped my boys and me. By the grace of God we escaped and he went to jail. Now you may think that this was the end but it wasn't. I still wanted to help him. I didn't oppose to him getting a bond. I thought that it would do more harm if he was incarcerated. Just 3 weeks after his release, he followed me to my boys' school and tried to kill us. His attempt failed and the threat that he scared me with months ago became reality. He committed suicide. See ladies, it never mattered how much I cared or loved, he was internally destroyed and broken. Nothing but prayer and God would've saved him. I'm not saying for you to stop loving or praying for your significant other, I'm saying that you must love yourself enough to not endure abuse in order for love to be reciprocated. You can still love and pray for them but remove yourself from the toxic environment.

Love doesn't hurt. Women we are settling and thus the epidemic of domestic violence and abuse continues to rise. Women we have to know our worth and know that if it feels wrong, 9 times out of 10, it is. The question was asked, "Why are abused women attracted to the same type of men?" This is my conclusion. Women who are abused are emotionally affected. When your emotions are not intact and you are in a vulnerable state and don't fully process the situation before entering another relationship, you are most likely to choose the same type of mate. I don't believe that this is a conscious decision but I do believe that it has more to do with "us" not properly healing our hearts. We must take the necessary time to repair and rebuild before moving on.

R. NIKKI CHANEY

I'm Strutting

Ladies the ultimate goal after enduring such traumatic experiences is rebuilding. Rebuild our self-esteem; rebuild our careers and rebuilding our lives, thus creating a fierce Strut. Our self-esteem is so damaged and needs to be fixed immediately. This is the first agenda that should be addressed. What is it ladies that gives you that confidence? What is it that you need to feel beautiful? For me, it was Heels. Have you ever heard of the famous quote by Marilyn Monroe, "Give a girl the right shoes and she can conquer the world." I applied that to my life. I picked up the pieces and began on my "Strut 2 Success." All the things that were taken from me, I began to reclaim. I enrolled in college in pursuit of a Master's Degree in Sports and Entertainment Law and began to surround myself around positive individuals. I took precious time out with my kids and began to offer them more of me, a happier mom. It doesn't happen overnight but God will see you through your journey. In 2012, I got the vision to start my own non-profit organization, Heel My Heart, Corporation, and I executed that vision as God birthed it into reality. I wanted to offer women an opportunity at rebuilding their lives by providing them an outlet that would encourage, empower and educate them. This is how I continue to get my "Strut On."

Ladies it was a pleasure to go on this journey with you and I thank you for allowing me to share my story. I pray that you will slide on your Heels and join me on this "Strut 2 Success." I'm *waiting on you so that we can complete this race together, S.T.R.U.T.ing (Sashaying Together Releasing Unapologetic Truths) in our heels. There is no need to apologize for your hurts, habits, or hang-ups. Stand in your truth. There is life after all the hurt and pain. We are SURVIVORS.*

STATE HOTLINES & COALITIONS

HEEL MY HEART, CORPORATION
PO BOX 3598 MCDONOUGH, GA 30253
PHONE: 404-426-0734
FAX: 770-288-3919
EMAIL: HEELMYHEART@GMAIL.COM
WEBSITE: WWW.HEELMYHEART.ORG

Alabama Coalition Against Domestic Violence
P.O. Box 4762
Montgomery, AL 36101
Phone: 1-800-650-6522 (in state)
Fax: 334-832-4803
TTY: 1-800-787-3224
Another State: 1-800-799-SAFE (7233)
Email: info@acadv.org
Crisis help lines are open 24 hours

Alaska Network on Domestic Violence and Sexual Assault
130 Seward Street, Room 214
Juneau, AK 99801
Phone: 907-586-3650
FAX: 907-463-4493
Hotline: 1-800-799-SAFE (7233)
lbrowne@andvsa.org

Arizona Coalition Against Domestic Violence
301 E. Bethany Home Rd.
Suite C194
Phoenix, AZ 85012
Phone: 602-279-2900
FAX: 602-279-2980
TTY: 602-279-7270
Toll-Free: 1-800-782-6400
E-mail: acadv@azcadv.org
Hours: 8:30am-5-00pm Monday - Friday

Arkansas Coalition Against Domestic Violence
1401 West Capitol Ave, Suite 170
Little Rock AR 72201
Phone: (501) 907-5612
FAX: (501)907-5618
Toll Free: (800)269-4668

Coalition to End Family Violence
1030 N. Ventra Rd
Oxnard, CA 93030
Phone: 805-983-6014
FAX: 805-983-6240
24-Hour Hotline: 805-656-1111

Spanish Hotline: 800-300-2181
TDD: 805-656-4439

Statewide California Coalition for Battered Women
PO Box 19005
Long Beach CA 90807
Toll-Free: 888-SCCBW-52
Phone: 562-981-1202
Fax: 562-981-3202
E-mail: sccbw@sccbw.org

Alternative Horizons
P.O. Box 503
Durango, CO 81302
Phone: 970-247-9619 (24-hour hotline)
E-mail: ah@frontier.net

Colorado Coalition Against Domestic Violence
1120 Lincoln Street, Suite 900
Denver, CO 80203
TOLL-FREE: 888-778-7091
Phone: 303-831-9632
FAX: 303-832-7067
E-mail: ccadv@ccadv.org

D.C. Coalition Against Domestic Violence
5 Thomas Circle, NW
Washington, DC 11005
Phone: 202-299-1181
FAX: 202-299-1193
E-mail: info@dccadv.org
Hours: 8:30am-5-00pm Monday - Friday

SOS Program (A part of DC Coalition)
Domestic Violence Intake Center Satellite Office
Greater Southeast Community Hospital
1328 Southern Ave SE
Room 311
Washington, DC 11032
Phone: 202-561-3095 x12
Fax: 202-561-3093
Hours: 9:00am-5:00pm

My Sister's Place
P.O. Box 29596
Washington, DC 11017
Phone: 202-529-5991 (24-hour hotline)
Administrative Office: 202-529-5261
Fax: 202-529-5984

Delaware Coalition Against Domestic Violence
100 W. 10th Street Suite 703
Wilmington, DE 19801
Phone: 302-658-2958
FAX: 302-658-5049
Hotline: 1-800-799-7233
E-mail: dcadv@dcadv.org

Florida Coalition Against Domestic Violence
425 Office Plaza Dr.
Tallahassee, FL 32301
TOLL-FREE: 800-500-1119
Phone: 850-425-2749
FAX: 850-425-3091
FL Domestic Violence Hotline: 1-800-500-1119
FL Domestic Violence Hotline TTY: 1-800-621-4202

Georgia Advocates for Battered Women and Children
250 Georgia Avenue, S.E., Suite 308
Atlanta, GA 30312
TOLL-FREE: 800-334-2836
Phone: 404-524-3847
FAX: 404-524-5959

Hawaii State Coalition Against Domestic Violence
716 Umi St., Unit 210
Honolulu, HI 96819
Phone: 808-832-9316
Fax: 808-841-6028
Email: hscadv@pixi.com

24 Hr Hawaii Shelters by Island:

- **Hilo:** 959-8864
- **Kauai:** 245-8404
- **Kona:** 322-SAFE (7233)
- **Maui/Lanai:** 579-9581
- **Molokai:** 567-6888
- **Oahu:** 841-0822

Iowa Coalition Against Domestic Violence
515 28th St
Suite 104
Des Moines, IA 50312
TOLL-FREE: 800-942-0333
Phone: 515-244-8028
FAX: 515-244-7417
E-mail: admin@icadv.org

Idaho Coalition Against Sexual and Domestic Violence
300 E. Mallard Dr., Suite 130
Boise, ID 83706
TOLL-FREE: 888-293-6118
Phone: 208-384-0419
FAX: 208-331-0687
E-mail: jmatshushita@idvsa.org

Illinois Coalition Against Domestic Violence
801 South 11th Street
Springfield, Illinios 62703
Phone: 217-789-2830
FAX: 217-789-1939
TTY: 217-241-0376
E-mail: ilcadv@springnet1.com

Between Friends
(Formerly The Friends of Battered Women and Their Children)
P. O. Box 608548
Chicago, IL 60660
Phone: 773-274-5232
FAX: 773-262-2543
HOTLINE: 1-800-603-HELP
E-mail:info@afriendsplace.org

Life Span
P.O. Box 1515
Des Plaines IL 60017
24-Hour Crisis Line: 847-824-4454
Phone: 847-824-0382
Fax: 847-824-5311
E-mail: life-span@life-span.org
Special site on Police Domestic Violence

Indiana Coalition Against Domestic Violence
1915 W. 18th Street, Suite B
Indianapolis, IN 46202
TOLL-FREE: 800-538-3393
Phone: 317-917-3685
Fax 317-917-3695
Crisis Line: 1-800-332-7385

Kansas Coalition Against Sexual and Domestic Violence
634 SW Harrison
Topeka, KS 66603
TOLL-FREE: 888-END-ABUSE (Kansas state-wide hotline)
Phone: 785-232-9784
FAX: 785-266-1874

Kentucky Domestic Violence Association
P.O. Box 356

R. NIKKI CHANEY

Frankfort, KY 40602
Phone: 502-209-5382
FAX: 502-226-5382
E-mail:info@kdva.org

Louisiana Coalition Against Domestic Violence
P.O. Box 77308
Baton Rouge, LA 70879-7308
Phone: 225-752-1296
FAX: 225-751-8927
HOTLINE: 1-888-411-1333

Maine Coalition to End Domestic Violence
170 Park St.
Bangor, ME 04401
Phone: 207-941-1194
FAX: 207-941-2327
HOTLINE: 866-83-4HELP
Email: info@mcedv.org

Maryland Network Against Domestic Violence
6911 Laurel Bowie Road, Suite 309
Bowie, MD 20715
TOLL-FREE: 800-MD-HELPS
Phone: 301-352-4574
FAX: 301-809-0422
Email: info@mnadv.org

Jane Doe Inc./Massachusetts Coalition Against Sexual Assault and Domestic Violence
14 Beacon Street, Suite 507
Boston, MA 02108
Phone: 617-248-0922
Crisis / Information: 989-686-4551
FAX: 617-248-0902
TTY/TDD: 617-263-2110
Email: info@janedoe.org

Bay County Women's Center
P.O. Box 1458
3411 E. Midland Rd.
Bay City, MI 48706
TOLL-FREE: 800-834-2098
Phone: 517-686-4551
FAX: 517-686-0906

Michigan 24-Hour Crisis Line: 517-265-6776

Minnesota Coalition for Battered Women
590 Park Street North, Suite 410

St. Paul, MN 55103
TOLL-FREE: 800-289-6177
Phone: 651-646-6177
FAX: 651-646-1527
E-mail: mcbw@pclink.com

Missouri Coalition Against Domestic Violence
217 Oscar Dr., Suite A
Jefferson City, MO 65101
Phone: 573-634-4161
FAX: 573-636-6613

Women's Support and Community Services
2165 Hampton Ave
St. Louis, MO 63139
HOTLINE: 314-531-1103
Office: 314-646-7500
Hours: Monday-Thursday 8:00am-7:00pm; Friday 8:00am-1:00pm

Mississippi State Coalition Against Domestic Violence
P.O. Box 4703
Jackson, MS 39296-4703
HOTLINE: 800-898-3234
After Hours HOTLINE: 1-800-799-7233
Phone: 601-981-9196
FAX: 601-981-2501
E-mail: mcadv@misnet.com
Hours: Monday-Friday 8:00am-5:00pm

Crisis Line
P.O. Box 6644
Great Falls, MT 59406
Phone: 406-453-HELP
TOLL-FREE: 1-888-587-0199

Montana Coalition Against Domestic and Sexual Violence
Montana Coalition Against Domestic & Sexual Violence
PO Box 818
Helena MT 59624
Phone: 406.443.7794
TOLL-FREE: 888-404-7794
Fax: 406.443.7818

Nebraska Domestic Violence and Sexual Assault Coalition
1000 "O" Street, Suite 102
Lincoln, NE 68508-2253
TOLL-FREE: 800-876-6238
Phone: 406-443-7794
FAX: 406-443-7818

Nevada Network Against Domestic Violence
220 S. Rock Blvd. Suite. 7
Reno , NV 89502
TOLL-FREE: 800-500-1556
Phone: 775-828-1115
FAX: 775-828-9991

Safe House
921 American Pacific Dr. Suite 300,
Henderson, NV 89014
Phone: 702-451-4203
FAX: 702-451-4302
HOTLINE: 702-564-3227
E-mail: kareng@safehouse.org

New Hampshire Coalition Against Domestic and Sexual Violence
P.O. Box 353
Concord, NH 03302-0353
TOLL-FREE For Domestic Violence: 866-644-3574
TOLL-FREE For Sexual Assault: 1-800-277-5570
Phone: 603-224-8893
Fax: 603-228-6096

New Jersey Coalition for Battered Women
1670 Whitehorse/Hamilton Square Road
Trenton, NJ 08690
TOLL-FREE: for Battered Lesbians: 800-224-0211 (in NJ only)
Phone: 609-584-8107
FAX: 609-584-9750
HOTLINE: 1-800-572-7233
TTY: 609-584-0027 (9am-5pm, then into message service)
E-mail: info@njcbw.org

Strengthen Our Sisters
P.O.Box U
Hewitt, N.J. 07421
HOTLINE: 800-SOS-9470 (800-767-9470)
Office: 973-248-0776
E-mail: info@sosdv.org

New Mexico State Coalition Against Domestic Violence
201 Coal Avenue SW
Albuquerque, NM 87102
TOLL-FREE: 800-773-3645 (in New Mexico Only)
Legal Helpline: 800-209-DVLH
Phone: 505-246-9240
FAX: 505-246-9434
E-mail: info@nmcadv.org

New York State Coalition Against Domestic Violence
350 New Scotland Avenue

Albany New York 12208
Phone: 518-482-5465
English: 1-800-942-6906
English TTY: 1-800-818-0656
Spanish: 1-800-942-6908
Spanish TTY: 1-800-780-7660
Fax: 518-482-3807
Email us at nyscadv@nyscadv.org

North Carolina Coalition Against Domestic Violence
123 W. Main Street, Suite 700
Durham, NC 27701
Phone: 919-956-9124
HOTLINE: 1-888-232-9124
FAX: 919-682-1449

Western Office:
PO Box 17398
Asheville, NC 28816
Phone: 828-505-3708

North Dakota Council on Abused Women's Services
State Networking Office
418 East Rosser Avenue, Suite 320
Bismarck, ND 58501
TOLL-FREE: 888-255-6240 (In ND Only)
Phone: 701-255-6240
FAX: 701-255-1904

Ohio Domestic Violence Network
4807 Evanswood Drive
Suite 201
Columbus, Ohio 43229
Phone: 614-781-9651
TTY: 614 781-9654
HOTLINE: 800-934-9840
Fax: 614 781-9652
E-mail: info@odvn.org

Oklahoma Coalition Against Domestic Violence and Sexual Assault
3815 N. Santa Fe Avenue, Suite 124
Oklahoma City, OK 73118
Telephone: 405-524-0700
Fax: 405-524-0711
E-mail: info@ocadvsa.org

Education Office:
PO Box 135
Poteau, OK 74953
Telephone: 918-647-5814
Fax: 918-649-3772

<u>Oregon Coalition Against Domestic Violence and Sexual Assault</u>
State Office:
380 Spokane St.
Suite 100
Portland, OR 97202
Telephone: 503-230-1951
TTY: 1-800-553-2508
Fax: 503-230-1973
Statewide Crisis Number: 1-888-235-5333

<u>Pennsylvania Coalition Against Domestic Violence/National Resource Center on Domestic Violence</u>
6440 Flank Drive, Suite 1300
Harrisburg, PA 17112-2778
Phone: 717-545-6400
Toll Free: 800-932-4632
TTY: 800-553-2508
FAX: 717-671-8149

<u>Women's Center of Montgomery County</u>
Main Administrative Office:
101 Washington Lane, Ste. WC-1
Jenkintown PA 19046
Toll-free hotline: 1-800-773-2424

Norristown Office:
Women's Advocacy Project
400 Courthouse Plaza, 18 W. Airy St.
Norristown PA 19404
610-279-1548

Pottstown Office:
Women's Advocacy Project
555 High Street, 2nd Floor
Pottstown PA 19464
610-970-7363

Bryn Mawr Office:
610-525-1427

Lansdale Office:
215-853-8060

<u>Laurel House</u>
P.O. Box 764
Norristown, PA 19404
Phone: 610-277-1860
HOTLINE: 1-800-642-3150
Fax: 610-277-64025
E-Mail: LaurelHaus@aol.com

HEEL MY HEART: MY STRUT 2 SUCCESS

Rhode Island Coalition Against Domestic Violence
422 Post Road, Suite 202
Warwick, RI 02888
HOTLINE: 800-494-8100
Phone: 401-467-9940
FAX: 401-467-9943
ricadv@ricadv.org

South Carolina Coalition Against Domestic Violence & Sexual Assault
(Link only works in Microsoft Internet Explorer)
P.O. Box 7776
Columbia, SC 29202-7776
TOLL-FREE: 800-260-9293
Phone: 803-256-2900
FAX: 803-256-1030

South Dakota Coalition Against Domestic Violence and Sexual Assault
P.O. Box 141
Pierre, SD 57501
HOTLINE: 800-430-7233
Phone: 605-945-0869
FAX: 605-945-0870

PO Box 1402
Sioux Falls, SD 57101
(605) 271-3171 Phone
(605) 271-3172 Fax
1-877-317-3096
(Info/Referral only)
Email: siouxfalls@sdcadvsa.org

Safe Harbor
PO Box 41
310 S. Kline St.
Aberdeen, SD 57402-0041
Phone: 605 226-1212
Toll Free: 888-290-2935
Fax: 650-226-2430
Email (general information only): safeharbor@safeharbor.ws

Tennessee Task Force Against Domestic Violence
2 International Plaza Dr., Suite 425
Nashville, TN 37217
TOLL-FREE: 800-289-9018
Phone: 615-386-9406
FAX: 615-383-2967
Email: webmistress@tcadsv.org

Texas Council on Family Violence
P.O. Box 161810
Austin, TX 78716

TOLL-FREE: 800-525-1978
Phone: 512-794-1133
FAX: 512-794-1199

Families In Crisis, Inc.
P.O. Box 25
Killeen, Texas 76540
Phone: 254-773-7765
Fax: 254-526-6111
HOTLINE: 888-799-SAFE

Domestic Violence Advisory Council
205 North 400 West
Salt Lake City, UT 84103
Phone: 801-521-5544
FAX: 801-521-5548

Women Helping Battered Women
PO BOX 1535
Burlington, VT
Phone: 802-658-3131
HOTLINE: 802-658-1996
TTY: 802-658-1996
Toll-free: 1-800-228-7395
E-mail: whbw@whbw.org

Women's Rape Crisis Center; Vermont
24 Hour HOTLINE: 802-863-1236
Statewide HOTLINE: 800-489-7273

Vermont Network Against Domestic Violence and Sexual Assault
P.O. Box 405
Montpelier, VT 05601
Phone: 802-223-1302
TTY: 800-223-1115
24 Hour HOTLINE: 1 800 228 7395
FAX: 802-223-6943
E-mail: info@vtnetwork.org

Virginians Family Violence and Sexual Assault Hotline

Charlottesville, VA
302 Hickman Rd
Suite 101
Charlottesville, VA 22911
Phone: 434-979-9002
Fax: 434-979-9003

Richmond, VA
5008 Monument Ave.

Suite A
Richmond, VA 23230
Phone: 804-377-0335
Fax: 804-377-0339
E-mail: info@vsdvalliance.org

Washington State Coalition Against Domestic Violence
WSCADV- Olympia Office
711 Capitol Way, Suite 702
Olympia, WA 98501
Phone: 360-586-1022
Fax: 360-586-1024
TTY: 360-586-1029

WSCADV - Seattle Office
1402 - 3rd Ave, Suite 406
Seattle WA 98101
206-389-2515
206-389-2520 FAX
206- 389-2900 TTY
E-mail: wscadv@wscadv.org

Washington State Domestic Violence Hotline
Tel: 800-562-6025
E-mail: csn@willapabay.org

West Virginia Coalition Against Domestic Violence
Elk Office Center
5004 Elk River Road,
Elkview, WV 25071
Phone: 304-965-3552
FAX: 304-965-3572

Manitowoc County Domestic Violence Center
1127 S. 22nd. St,
Manitowoc, WI 54220
Phone: 920-684-5770
HOTLINE: 877-275-6888
Fax:920-684-6344
E-mail: dvc@sbcglobal.net

Wisconsin Coalition Against Domestic Violence
307 S. Paterson St. #1
Madison, WI 53703
Phone: 608-255-0539
Fax: 608-255-3560

Wyoming Coalition Against Domestic Violence and Sexual Assault
P.O. Box 236
Laramie, WY 82073

R. NIKKI CHANEY

TOLL-FREE: 800-990-3877
Phone: 307-755-5481
Legal Staff: 307-755-0992
Fax: 307-755-5482
E-mail: msholtywcadvsa@yahoo.com

YWCA Battered Women Task Force-Topeka
225 SW 12th St.
Topeka, KS 66612
Daytime: 785-354-7927
Evening and Weekend: 785-234-3300
24 Hour HOTLINE : 1-888-822-2983
Hours: Monday, Wednesday,Thursday and Friday:8:00am-4:30pm; Tuesday 10:30am-4:30pm

ABOUT THE AUTHOR

Author and Philanthropist R. Nikki Chaney overcame over a decade of domestic violence and abuse. Two novels precede this self-help journal, and are available for purchase through the company's website www.heelmyheart.org. She continues to inspire and empower women through her words and also through Heel My Heart, Corporation. Continue to support Author Chaney on her journey to empower, encourage, and educate women affected by domestic violence and abuse.

Connect with us

**HEEL MY HEART
NIKKI HARRISON FANPAGE**

**HEEL MY HEART
STRUT 2 SUCCESS**

HEELS4ACAUSE

R. NIKKI CHANEY

www.ingramcontent.com/pod-product-compliance
Lightning Source LLC
Chambersburg PA
CBHW060427050426
42449CB00009B/2170